Compositions on Compassion and Other Emotions

Essays, Illustrations, Poems,
and Short Stories
by Bob McNeil

Flexible Press
Minneapolis, Minnesota 2023

Print ISBN: 979-8-9862459-8-0
eBook ISBN: 979-8-9862459-9-7

Editor: Ed Sheehy
Flexible Press LLC
Book design: William Burleson
Cover Art: Bob McNeil and Yul Miller
Illustrations and photos: Bob McNeil
Except for "DJ at Night" and "Still Thinking"
by Yul Miller, dedication page and page 82
"Jazz Singer" and "Betty Grable"
by Howard McNeil, pages 35 and 42
and a collage by J.E.M. Jones, page 55

Portions of this book originally appeared in the *Hope Anthology, Autumn Noir: An Unsettling Reads Anthology; The Impressment Gang Issue 2:3; New Reader Magazine; Pinnacle: A Poetry Anthology; The Quilled Ink Review Volume 1 Ode to Love; Int'l Beat Poetry Foundation Goddess Anthology 2022: Poets Celebrating Women; Continue the Voice Issue 15: Celebration, Self-Portrait Poetry Collection (Silver Birch Press Anthologies Volume 10); Lyrics of Mature Hearts: A Poetry Anthology; San Francisco Peace and Hope Literary Arts Journal; The Borfski Press Issue IV; Spectrum: A Colorful Collection of SmartyPants' Best; Glacial Hills Review: Summer 2022; The Authors Porch Issue # 5 Beyond The Call; New Generation Beats: National Beat Poetry Foundation, Inc. 2022 Anthology;* and *Inner Child Press International Poetry, the Best of 2022 Anthology.*

To Yul Miller, my late friend
who worked on his art every night
back when I did not know what to do with any given hour.
Seeing him by his window and drafting board
gave me a rudder that prevented my creativity from drifting aimlessly.

Foreword

People who are my contemporaries or older will remember that cigarettes seemed pleasant and fashionable years ago. Both off and on stage, various singers moved nicotine to their lips often. Classic films, namely *Now, Voyager*, made smoking romantic. Sidney Poitier showed me a cool style of lighting a cig in *Raisin in the Sun*.

Life at home verified that smoking posed no hardship. My responsible, hardworking father favored Belair. Numerous hours as a mutuel teller at Belmont, Aqueduct, or Saratoga racetracks ended with Martinis and his butts of choice. Without a tail, I approximated the behavior of a dutiful dog and brought his beverage. My servile service, by age 12, had a perk. His postprandial somnolence and inebriation made it easy for me to steal his mentholated pacifiers.

Subsequent decades passed, and I was up to two packs a day. Either I rode filtered Camels or the Marlboro Man's horse. Both the trip and the destination commandeered every moment. Mornings started with tobacco in my lungs. Meals never seemed complete without inhaling noxious pillows. Intimacy with a partner required a few drags after an orgasm. Surpassing a food-related hunger, my need for breathable poison continued. Neither my father's death due to cancer nor a friend's emphysema-caused demise stopped the ongoing oral obsession.

Around age 39, I got an offer from a Haitian opera singer named Martine Bruno. She asked me to read arias in English after she sang them during a concert. My poetry recital experience gave me a method for handling the show at the Grace Congregational Church of Harlem. The Goddess *Meret* blessed that singer's throat. Attendees with working ears loved her every utterance. Monolingual individuals had no clue what she was singing in Italian. They awaited my translation. I gave the show the bravado of Mighty Mouse, and my unsubtle performance received a favorable response.

My throat's reaction to the recitation did not fare that well after the program ended. It had the force of a conflagration. Rafter-smashing bombast came back to bite me in the trachea. I was sure the imagined flames would create a hole in my neck. Furthermore, indications seemed to point toward me using an electrolarynx. Insensitive folks called it a cancer kazoo. Contemplating that state motivated the best action in my life thus far. I decided to unhitch myself from cancer sticks.

Giving up a chemical dependency seemed tantamount to cutting off an appendage. Something made me employ the ablactation process. That is, my mouth could no longer suck nicotine tits forty times a day. Untutored but determined, I figured maybe trying lighter cigarettes would help too. It did. Consequently, I used the nicotine patch. Believe it or not, it worked.

For fifteen years, I enjoyed not having my lungs filled with pollution. Everything about me got reborn. I had a teenager's stamina. Thus purified, I preached about better health to my friends. I got so strong that partying with the most ardent smokers had zero effect on me. Distant from temptation, I remained tenacious.

Right up with hearing a politician tell the truth and thieves returning stolen goods, the unexpected happened. I started coughing incessantly. Playing doctor in my youth did not provide a clue about my condition. I believed a cold or COVID-19 came to kill me. Dosing myself with antihistamines seemed reasonable. But Edna, a good friend, insisted I go to the hospital. Grudgingly, I went.

In the medical facility, I learned that my end was nigh. The physicians gave my enemy a name. They called it tension pneumothorax. My right lung approximated the behavior of a flat tire and deflated. Worse still, it pressed against my heart. Delaying my operation would have only made a mortician happy.

Oddly enough, a pending meeting with the Reaper inspired no regret. Not completing another manuscript terrified me. Bedridden with three tubes draining my lung, I gathered my writing and illustrations mentally in the hope of leaving a testimonial.

Although the operation was successful, the medical staff warned me about a potential relapse. Unremittingly at home, I worked on this dream book. Lacking a seer's sight, I never thought the bound and published version would ever come to fruition.

Syncretism defines this collection of words and images. The volume conveys my opinion that myriad beliefs have value. They are doors leading to spiritual fortification. On these pages, you will find various philosophies conversing without conflict. By means of this eclectic approach, I hope the amalgamation will create a better appreciation between others and myself. Moreover, the fact that proceeds from this well-meaning work will fund a homeless organization gives my need to breathe greater purpose. Knowing my simple creations can help others is the most satisfying addiction.

>Bob McNeil
>Bridgeport, CT

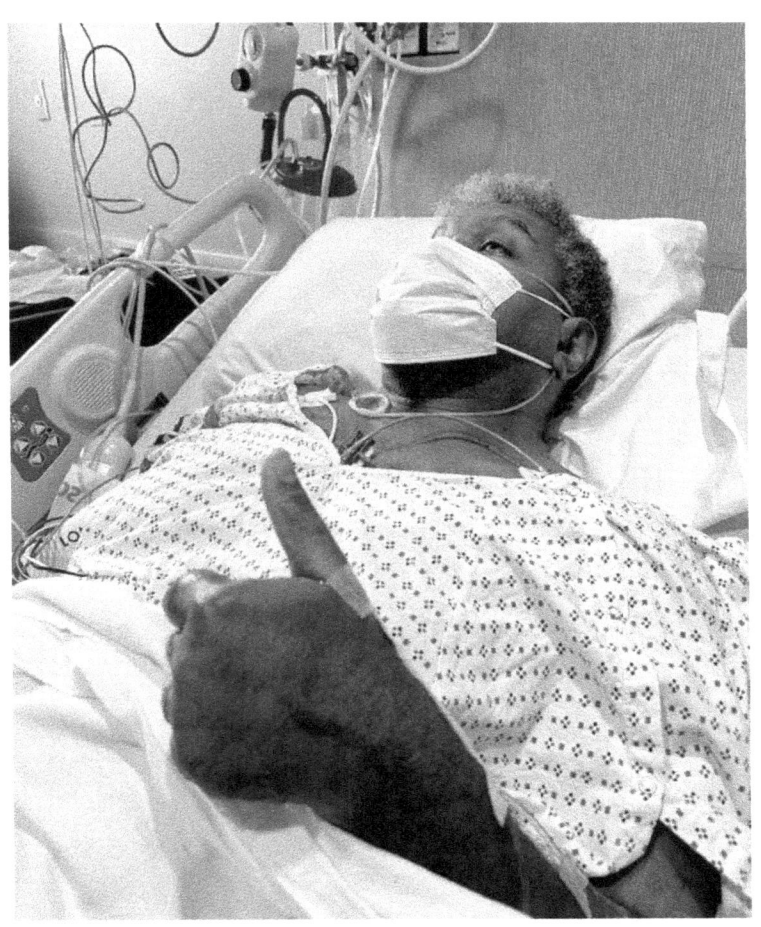

Download
an
Upward View

An Introduction

No matter at what moment you refer to the news, either on television or the internet, you will find hatred and violence in myriad forms on local or global levels. They are omnipresent. And to make matters even worse, a pandemic made the irate more ireful.

These pestiferous times tested the strength of families, marriages, and other relationships. Our lives got packed up. Many existences could not survive confinement. Stress tore apart formerly tensile ties, leaving battered baggage.

Under modern life's blitz attack on the Earth and its inhabitants, we require love and hope. Those emotions provide nutrients for individuals who crave optimism. Amid innumerable maladies, we must try to love others with ardor. In defiance of how dark and dire existence gets, we must continue hoping there will be an era of illuminating betterment.

Many selections in this book deal with the importance of love and hope. However, without question, cynics will say these sentiments seem better suited for art than everyday existence. They may argue that devotion to these desires is on par with a belief in flying horses. Nevertheless, the words in this collection humbly express how faith and affection are building blocks that require brick-strong dedication. Without these components, there would be no place to house the best aspects of our humanity.

The Eternal Recurrence

"The eternal hourglass of existence is turned upside down again and again, and you with it, speck of dust!"—Nietzsche

To date, our planet
is a burning skillet.
*Amor fati.**
Battle after battle
reduces us to cattle.
Amor fati.
And there is a virus
analogous to any serial killer among us.
Amor fati.
Throughout the distress and injustice,
embrace those you lustfully trust.
Amor fati.
Treat your every Eros-blest passion
with a condemned person's dedication
who's hours from execution.
Amor fati.
Once the door of the world
comes off its mechanism,
glee is the adhesive
for such a schism.
Amor fati.

* Amor fati: Latin for love of fate.

What Hope Evokes

Although old hope seems notional

as a picture of God's features,

a supposed space saucer in the Nevada area,

a purported attention bid from a cryptid,

a research-devoid tabloid, or a storefront psychic,

we want a dose of it when downhearted or sick.

Previous to the Apocalypse

Yet again,

fellow survivors,

much to an apocalypticist's

dismay,

we persevered

through another

year's worth

of earthly curses

that dispersed storms,

quakes, plagues,

and blood-pouring wars.

Go celebrate

the terrestrial expo

by doing shenanigans

that summon

your disposition's

harlequin.

Identical to Wite-Out

plied on ink,

unthink

your hate.

Then link

with your lovable mate.

Turn to the troposphere

and toast

to a time

when existence is

not fraught

with a savage tonnage.

My Heart's Unthwarted Sentiment

Captcha,

here is my answer:

I am

regrettably

mortal,

although I wish

a combination

of wires

and programs

could uninstall

all memories

of humankind's

unkindness.

Commuting Into Myself

The fare to ride
this cerebral subway is
increasing.
Commuting into myself
reveals train tracks
are my bones,
third rails
serve the nervous system,
and hungry rats
encapsulate this disposition.

Superego Transit Cops believe
these reactions could be
terrorist cells.
They check the bags
beneath my eyes,
considering if that's where
I keep my pipe bomb visions.

My ill temper repeatedly transfers
from train to train.
Sure enough,
my neurosis out growls
the underground system
with each delay.
Derelict aspirations panhandle,
pleading to get pleasure,
and my other rush-hour-big bipolar hordes
can't fit their problems
through the exits.

The Inner Voice
Address System
apologizes for the traffic
up ahead.
It explains why
turtles in a tar pit
would be better at transporting
me to my destination.

Ever a philomath,
I inspect the transit map
and seek life's right station.
Perhaps on the next ride,
I'll find it.

Download an Upward View

Press Esc
When your Thoughtfulness Program
Won't open, or
Press Control, Alt, and Delete
If still stuck
In a rancor-mannered mode.

Log out of demagoguery.
Reboot your benevolence
Anytime intolerance
Attaches itself
With a spam virus's
Tenaciousness.

Wait, then
Log into something humane.
Use your Solicitude App
To ensure it won't happen again.

Parranda

Wear a mask
and let your eyes
loudly say what your mouth won't.
Stand six feet apart,
imparting sentences
that embrace those you love.
Then self-isolate.
That insulated time is a coat
during a life-endangering storm.
Start a party within yourself.
Sing the lyric your spirit wrote.
Don't let anything
silence your celebration.
Welcome gladness,
your venerated guest.

An Empedoclean Dream

Over the centuries, I've been a bird back when

air owned the sweetness of any gourd grown,

a tree while generations grew beneath me,

moss on a mountain noted for titanic magnificence,

a slug slithering aimlessly without a smidgen of sentience,

and a man who dreamt of a world with better humans.

Of those incarnations, I loathed that last transformation the most.

Praise for My Forebears

Sent on ships with shark-rancorous crews
   That beat human beings
   Until blood bombarded the decks,
   My stolen, worry-swollen
   Brethren defied tragedy's tide
   And revivified pride by surviving.
Years of lash-and-gash chattel anguish
   Inspired ire comparable to hellfire.
   In between the sorrow
   And plots to deal thralldom a deathblow,
   My prayer-sending brethren
   Defied tragedy's tide
   And revivified pride by surviving.
Raging pages of centuries turned,
   And Cain-hateful conflicts burned,
   Revealing uncivil evil,
   A Republic's upheaval.
   Even so, my burden-beset brethren
   Defied tragedy's tide
   And revivified pride by surviving.
Across that battered habitat,
   Beings and things shook
   And took soldiers to disaster-laid graves.
   But my brethren's value-engraved resource,
   Courageous will, was saved.
   Again, they defied tragedy's tide
   And revivified pride by surviving.
No matter the conflict's length,
   My brethren possessed a mountain's strength.

The Borough Where Liberty Flowed

1.

Long ago, tribes trod this land of mine. I heard their praise songs for the sun, air, and soil. Atop my anatomy's north side, Matinecocks resided. Whereas on the south side, Marsapeagues dwelled. Throughout my anatomy's quintessence, I treasured them both. Each spring-warm hour had flowering beauty, and I believed you were bees desiring my pistils.

2.

Recollections of the 1600s, on the order of galleons sailing, return to me. Aliens arrived without an invitation and called my acres home. Whilst my apprehension about the invasion grew, the Dutch governed and townships formed. Following that, the English named me after Queen Catherine of Braganza.

3.

In the 1700s, cannons sent warring spheres to your former land's armies. And I prayed that democracy would come for everyone, ending years of dread and finally letting love wed hearts. I waited until you understood the meaning of equality.

4.

Eon upon eon, I watched the detestable sadness and madness of oppressiveness. Some peace surfaced once you Quakers and other ethical ponderers around the 1800s followed heaven's behavior and used the land I am for what you called the Underground Railroad. My landscape assisted the escape of runaway slaves. Watching democracy rebirth itself gave my earth the nutrition it needed.

5.

Now let's bless time's progress. The 1900s brought more immigrants to me and the four adjacent family points. Every land's culture provided another color for our canvas. And this nation, with my borough in tow, wanted to defeat Mercury's speed. First, the horses, then carriages, trains, automobiles, and planes provided motion on and above my terrain. Comets should have known awe once they saw my children's speed. You drank from the Well of Cleverness. The more you hydrated, the more you created. Hence, aerials, antennas, satellites, and computers made information air-accessible.

6.

Out of my womb's terrain, fame became a forest. I birthed laudable and questionable politicians, gifted actors, singers, rappers, and rockers. Quite a few enthusiasts prefer to recall how Rock 'n' Roll outraced the Blues. But my Astoria, Bayside, Cambria Heights, Corona, East Elmhurst, Elmhurst, Flushing, Forest Hills, Hollis, Jackson Heights, Jamaica, St. Albans, Springfield Gardens, and Sunnyside remember the jazz of Bennett, Corea, Armstrong, Gillespie, Holiday, Goodman, Miller, Coltrane, Fitzgerald, and Horne residing in the borough that I am.

7.

Within this century and every epoch after it, my words and deeds will forever serve you, my children: my Chinese, Japanese, Vietnamese, Korean, and Filipino children; my Bangladeshi, Nepali, and Pakistani children; my Native American, African American, Central American, South American, Dominican, Mexican, and Puerto Rican children; and my Irish, Polish, Italian, and Russian children. My children, these verses do not mention every citizen who brightens the borough that I am; nonetheless, this well-meaning ode is for anyone who makes me their abode.

What
Love
Wrote

What Love Wrote

Of the subjects at a writer's disposal, love is perhaps the most popular. Quite amazingly, despite wars, famine, economic strife, and this planet's ravenous necrogenic appetite, the topic endures. From schoolchildren to scholars, love is a favored premise in verse.

Under the conditions of pain, rejection, and loneliness, writers can appreciate Eros, Philia, Ludus, Agape, Pragma, Philautia, and Storge. Case in point: try to imagine monarchy-massive wealth. If life blessed you with every lavish resource, you would tire of the opulence. Let's say with that money, you could eat white Alba truffles anytime. After a while, you would no longer appreciate the flavor or texture of the tubers. The food would become quite trite. It would be soporific indeed. This, too, could be said of love. If your every desire is satisfied all the time, you will learn to take it for granted. Now and then, you hear couples use this phrase: He or she does not appreciate me anymore. Alas, to quote Shakespeare, "Ay, there's the rub."

Here's another example: Robert and Elizabeth Browning's poems articulate love effectively because of the hardships they overcame. Their connubial union was fate's gift after anguished years. Elizabeth's illness and her father's disapproval of her romantic relationship did not impede her love for Robert. Filled with affection, respect, and words, the Brownings created a union for the ages.

Always remember that in our world of inexhaustible unpleasantness, there is the beauty of love. This point did not elude the Brownings, and it must not get lost on us either.

Sequestered With You

(for Edna Garcia)

It matters less
now that dark curtains
veil our view.
In isolation,
days—elliptical as haiku—
end quickly,
yet our nights
scroll out to an epic length.
The season dons dour hues
that contrast
with the carnival-celebratory shades
dancing to our upbeat bond.
Long before the seasonal coldness,
the world became frigid from fear.
Under the covers,
our oasis,
we kiss
and disregard every part
of the outside.

Regarding Reality in the Morning Light

Cramped on the couch
in my girlfriend's apartment,
a fear of knocking a cabinet
filled with flower-beautiful,
glass-fragile knickknacks stirred me.
Or was it the radio announcer
talking about COVID-19
killing more individuals
than the single-engine dive bombers
over Pearl Harbor on December 7
that startled me?
Or was it the aromatic java
summoning a reality
in need of Dionysian dreams
that roused me?
Or was it the sight of you,
my companion, wearing a mask
that made me welcome wakefulness again?
Such a vision proved how,
even during a quarantine,
nothing could obscure your beauty.

Unfinished Wishes

Within our thoughts,
we each have a love poem
that's so profound.
Nine muses would ponder it.

Within our thoughts,
we each have a love song
that's so honeyed.
Birds would mimic facets.

Within our thoughts,
we each have a tribute to love
that's so touching.
We'll go on creating it
until our obits are writ.

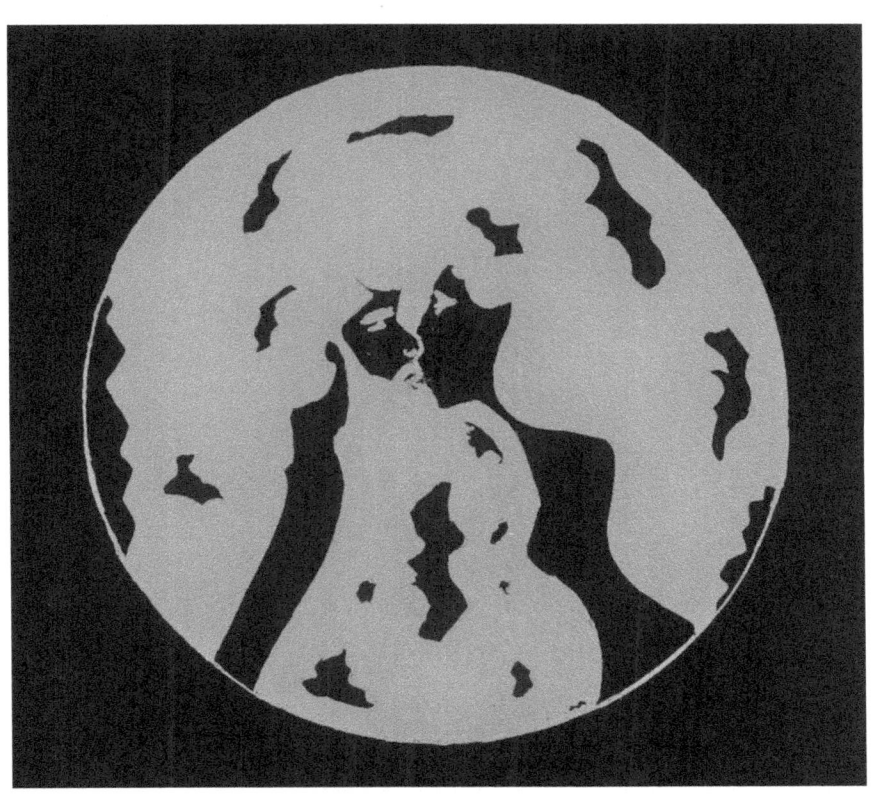

A Nocturnal Confessional

Luna after luna,
alma gemela,
I relive a previous grievance.
Quarrelsome things you said
stayed cemented,
paving over better sentiments.

Amid lucidity,
I realize antagonists attract.
That is why
I offer this verse
of reconciliation.

Let's walk
along our war's wreckage,
salvage pieces of our lives
once shared,
and build
a stone-stable sanctuary
to harbor
our oft-desired peace
together.

Our Parts of Which We Speak

I enjoy how your verbs
    taste, stroke, and titillate
    my flesh and soul.

I endure your adjectives'
    desire to describe the details of beauty.
    Adjectives are paintings of dawn:
    they strike sulfur,
    but they do not emblazon my vision with brilliance.

I revere the nouns that name
    the person, place, and thing that you are.
    Every appellation I use provides
    another reference to the benevolence of you.

I hate the pronouns assigned to design ourselves,
    for wrapping yourself in pink
    won't disguise the cries of your mannish side,
    and my anima is pregnant with a passion to reproduce.

I appreciate the conjunction that you have grown to be.
    You are the "and" that facilitates my spirit's state
    by using the adhesion of compassion.

I adore you for the prepositions that grant these facts:

    I am on a bed of beatitude with you.

    We do what we want for joy's geysers

    to experience satisfaction after the flow.

I titter at the interjections

    we use for illustrations of our jubilation.

    The exclamations are sillier

    than children chortling on a carousel.

I assert adverbially

    that both you and I have become

    rather devoted to the notion

    of cherishing an emotion

    without using its word.

    Soundlessly appreciating a thoughtful space

    waiting for language to transport the topic,

    our best sentiments on commitment get expressed.

Archived

Short-term memory loss is similar
to watching TV commercials.
The memories ask for my attention,
only to lose it with the next
round of remembrances.
Other times, that loss of short-term memory
reminds me of movie trailers.
Although the memories are loud
and lavishly bright with self-importance,
they leave no inerasable image.
Sometimes short-term memories
can appear like billboards
across an express train window,
flashing briefly as the locomotive
moves to the next station.
At this station of my life,
I am content just having a long-term
memory of once loving you.

Jazlynn

Via a Harlem Hotel window,
I heard the day
imitate "Rhapsody in Blue."
One clarinet wheeled in howling;
later, rush-hour notes
from saxophones, trumpets,
woodwinds, and violins.
Besides their vehicular tonality,
additional instruments
aroused my tympanum.

Then the day swung to another rhythm,
and its Chick-Webb-fast drumming life
was beckoning my feet.
Opposing my slow drag dance mood,
the alarm yelled,
"Since Duke Ellington's A Train
won't nap,
out tap the Nicholas Brothers
and do Cab Calloway's 'Jumpin Jive.'"

On a queen-sized bed,
an Oshun*-picturesque seductress,
who should have been
Billie Holiday's twin,
said hello in that way good gin
gets you.
Inebriated by everything she stated,
I heard her say,
"In our jam,
you grooved well,
real well,

but don't exit
until after your encore kisses,
crooner."

My response was raspy,
similar to Louis Armstrong's exuberance
when he sang "Hello, Dolly."
A few coughs into my sentence,
my voice became Chet Baker's.

Either the coffee
or her kisses
made my hangover
recede, and it revealed
her name.
Her name was Jazlynn,
but she preferred
the pizzazz of the tag
"Jazz."

* Oshun: A Goddess in the Yoruba religion who controls love and wealth, etc.

The Interval
of
All Things
Fantastical

The Pincushion

My second-grade teacher, who reminded me of Endora on *Bewitched*, gave an odd assignment to make pincushions. For an unfathomable reason, she thought sharp scissors, sewing needles, threads, happy-face-adorned fabrics, and cotton were beneficial for young boys and girls. Do I have to tell you how many kids in my classroom cut themselves? Band-Aids and cheerleader encouragement kept us laboring with the zeal of sweatshop employees. Had the calendar not told me it was the decade of my fashionably big afro and bellbottom jeans, I would have assumed we resided in the time of thralldom.

Shockingly, despite a propensity for clumsiness, I didn't hurt myself on a physical level. My self-respect got shorn, though. The pincushion I made had the appearance of a dog's chew toy. Other students did not experience this inadequacy. Their work had what mine lacked, which was competence.

The bell, at last, rang. I grabbed my gear, composed of a notebook, a Super Friends lunchbox, and a puke-green corduroy jacket. Close to my skips, there was the very thing I wanted. A perfectly formed pincushion waited for me on the floor. It had the look of a product straight out of a store. Exhibiting the deftness of a shoplifter, I retrieved the item. Stealing it from another student did not disturb me. Getting caught did.

Jesse Owens would have marveled at the speed I used when exiting the room. Believe me, I was not in a rush to get home. Seeing cartoons, *Dark Shadows*, and *The Wild Wild West* could wait for another day. Escaping with my prize had true importance.

With great zeal, I wanted my home's confines. Thankfully, the cheese-yellow school bus sliced through the traffic and took me to Wonder-Bread-soft comfort. Right at the point, the commute ended, I ran inside the house, yelling, "Mommy, look what I made for you."

Mother brushed her Cher-similar hair back and served a toasty kiss on my cheek. She stared at the pincushion, and her attitude possessed the illumination I needed. That radiance was worthy of a Polaroid SX-70 Land Camera photo.

"You really made this for me. It's beautiful," she said in a voice that should have been on an LP record or an 8-track tape.

I relished receiving royal reverence in our Queens, New York, home. Everything in me wanted to provide a response that would make my mother love my efforts forever. But a disturbing thing happened between my brain and mouth. The fib I wanted to tell got arrested in my throat by a Dick-Tracy-moralistic detective. Flooded by such a character's imaginary interrogation lamp, my untruth got a sermon about honesty. Instead of my intended words, a confession with the ease of egg yolk spilled out.

"I lied. Another kid made it."

Mom did not need a mood ring for me to know how she felt. Her complexion acquired a lava lamp's redness with a pet rock's countenance.

Prior to and after dinner, I got reprimanded. In lieu of my mother's resentment, I wanted praise for honesty. Adulation should have had the sweetness of a Watergate Salad or a 7 Up. The criticism I received boarded on the kale's bitterness atop my plate.

Many decades have passed since that incident. Nonetheless, the pincushion haunts all of my creative endeavors. To this day, it reminds me never to plagiarize. My creations may lack a tailor's precision, but they are always mine.

Blessed Meals During Cursed Times

Holding the same Biblical urge
To end barbarity's scourge,
My antebellum ancestors
Prayed a rescuer would emerge.

Left beside their regrets,
They sought manna for their palates.
And there was a seasoned trove
Over an ebony mama's stove.

If you ate their edibles,
Existence felt palatable.
Punches got munched apart.
They fried, sautéed, or baked,
And many aches went away.

Mamas' recipes sent servitude's hurts
Past tyranny's outskirts.
Seeing gladness protrude,
They gave nutrition to various broods.
Considering the fortifiers served,
Those ladies deserved grateful words.

Of Cinema and Nostalgia

Previous to VHS, DVR, and TV stations that rival the number of plants in a forest, people used to wake up or stay up for all sorts of movies and programs. My father, a cinephile, often woke me during the wee hours of a summer night to watch old films. He had a fondness for Betty Grable. On seeing her legs, I agreed with his fixation. Also, I thought only Bogart and Dad looked cool in a fedora and trench coat.

A Mantra for Babas

(Inspired by my Beloved Dad who raised me)

Many can father,

Yet select dads stay.

Select dads labor.

Select dads

Quash any mammoth-strong wrongness

That threatens who they begat.

Many can father,

Yet select dads stay.

Select dads labor.

Select dads

Stop any bladed vice

Attempting to slice kindred life.

Many can father,

Yet select dads stay.

Select dads labor.

Select dads

Gladly let their deeds

Feed their families' moral creeds.

Lessons I Took in Brooklyn

(for Ray Lewis)

Exceeding the heedlessness of a housepet set free,
I played in my Bed-Stuy neighborhood.
The asphalt was a field for sports.
Concrete made the recreation area complete.
Hydrants formed fountains and flumes
with flowing barrels of heat-deleting miracles.
A bent back became London Bridge.
Used bottle caps never made it to the garbage.
They were repositories for wax
and skill in skelly.
Broomsticks or mop handles
supplied the equipment for a tournament.

Perched with falcon eyes,
window-set mommies and grandmommies
knew everybody's names and families.
And if kids did bad things,
words about those misdeeds
flew to homes
and waiting belts.

The slap-sobering reality
was that our ghetto
never seemed woeful.
Nothing I wanted or cared to see
resided beyond it.

Granted, the world is vast,
but it will never surpass
the memories I amassed
during those years past.

The Interval of All Things Fantastical

(for Avery Jones-McNeil)

Son,
During my grasshopper-fast days,
I radiated sunrays.
Out and about the family's chocolate house,
Harlequin-grinning,
My hours spent were cartoon-polychromatic and quixotic.

Beatitude was a bonbon I chewed on
Between speaking a self-made tongue
To an imaginary friend for fun.
I drew a few fridge-bound heroes,
Then staged sci-fi scenes with action figurines.
And by donning a sheet, I became super undefeatable.

When outside, I had the grace of a wing
On a park swing,
Surveying the glory of everything.
Under Ra's radiating embrace,
I claimed the gold-holding clouds
And made them my own.

Son,
Now it's your time to climb giant dreams
While I vicariously watch fantasies lift you
To the level of a wind-drifting leaf.
Through you, my heart is youthful again,
And days are buttercups glazed
With the sweetest taste
That make me ignore what's in store
For your bitterly mature years ahead.

Sentiments
Before Residence
in the Firmament

A Mouse and the Lack of Housing

Sad to say, there was a death on the eighth floor of the 30th Street Men's Shelter in Manhattan. A mouse wound up dead in the stairwell. Mice, roaches, and bedbugs in this HRA are common. Therefore, a deceased rodent did not surprise anyone. The reaction to the passing trapped my imagination in glue.

Two middle-aged security guards, one black and one white, saw the 10-cm mouse. Both found the notion of picking up the critter repugnant. Neither got a broom, either. What they agreed upon was kicking the creature to another floor. Other staff members, specifically the custodians and administrators, and shelter residents reveled in booting the thing down the stairs.

The dead mass of hair and tail reached the first floor, where it met a sugar-alabaster woman with a vinegar-sour demeanor. Fastidious to the point of seeming militaristic, she yelled, "My job is not cleaning up dead mice. I need a porter who can sweep this thing up from here now, damn it, right this second."

Eventually, thanks to an unseen custodial worker, the creature found its necropolis in a garbage can. That mouse was a metaphor for the homeless in major cities and elsewhere. Thousands suffer under the same systemic method. Displaced masses get tossed around the system with no care. They only end up dead in bureaucratic trash, waiting for a real economic solution.

Both my grandmothers, back when I was younger, talked about a person who would have probably cared about that mouse and those individuals without housing. They said he quit his carpentry career. Unconcerned with legal tender, he did not pay taxes. Contrary to the advice of certain peers, he declared respect for a Lord no one could see. Their tale makes me wonder how the system would treat that man if he were poor, sick, and dying in a men's shelter stairwell.

Sentiments Before Residence in the Firmament

Aging is an express train that expresses no interest in our comprehension of the commute. We enter a world that transports us to the last stop, never stopping to ask if we want a longer journey. Demise pays for the ride. That point seems clear after leaving a loved one at their line's end.

So on this journey, share the assets of your time, praising those you love and respect. Withdraw valued sentiments from the bank of your heart. Transfer them to meaningful mortals. Do it soon. The counting house has finite hours.

Whatever the day, be it your birthday, a holiday, or just a regular weekday, I want everybody holding this page to know your existence is cherishable to me every day.

A Belated Blazon of Passion

(for Patricia Landrum)

Imagistic sister,
you were dawn-beautiful
and flower-delightful,
sailing sweetly
on New York streets.
Oh, you gold-hued
Queen, clad in velvet midnight
with neon-colored fingernails,
I adored seeing your cinnamon
and yellow jasmine
feather-soft tresses
sway around this town.

Sappho's odes,
 Giovanni's Black ire,
Dickinson's indigo ideas,
and Walker's purple truths
resided in your mind,
imagistic sister.
Calliope guided your genius,
and your conceptual comets
blazed and amazed
the horizon in my head.

Employing the skill of a healer,

I wanted to touch you

coo-soothingly,

imagistic sister.

But you died,

leaving unrequited hearts

desiring a caress

that never coalesced.

Housed in the Heaven

of my vision,

you will forever remain

dawn-beautiful

and flower-delightful.

The Pages That Made Us
(for J.E.M. Jones)

Our relationship,

always a product

of words upon pages,

was ink

that printed love letters and poems.

Each verse or billet-doux

gave our existence a reason

for existing together.

Written or typed,

they joined

other forms of memorabilia

in manila folders.

This year,

atop the files,

sits your obituary.

That page falls short

of defining your Isis-wise insights.

Your death notice

awaits my long-awaited

death notice,

which will be a bookend

for our book's end,

a dénouement lined

with our hypergraphic lives.

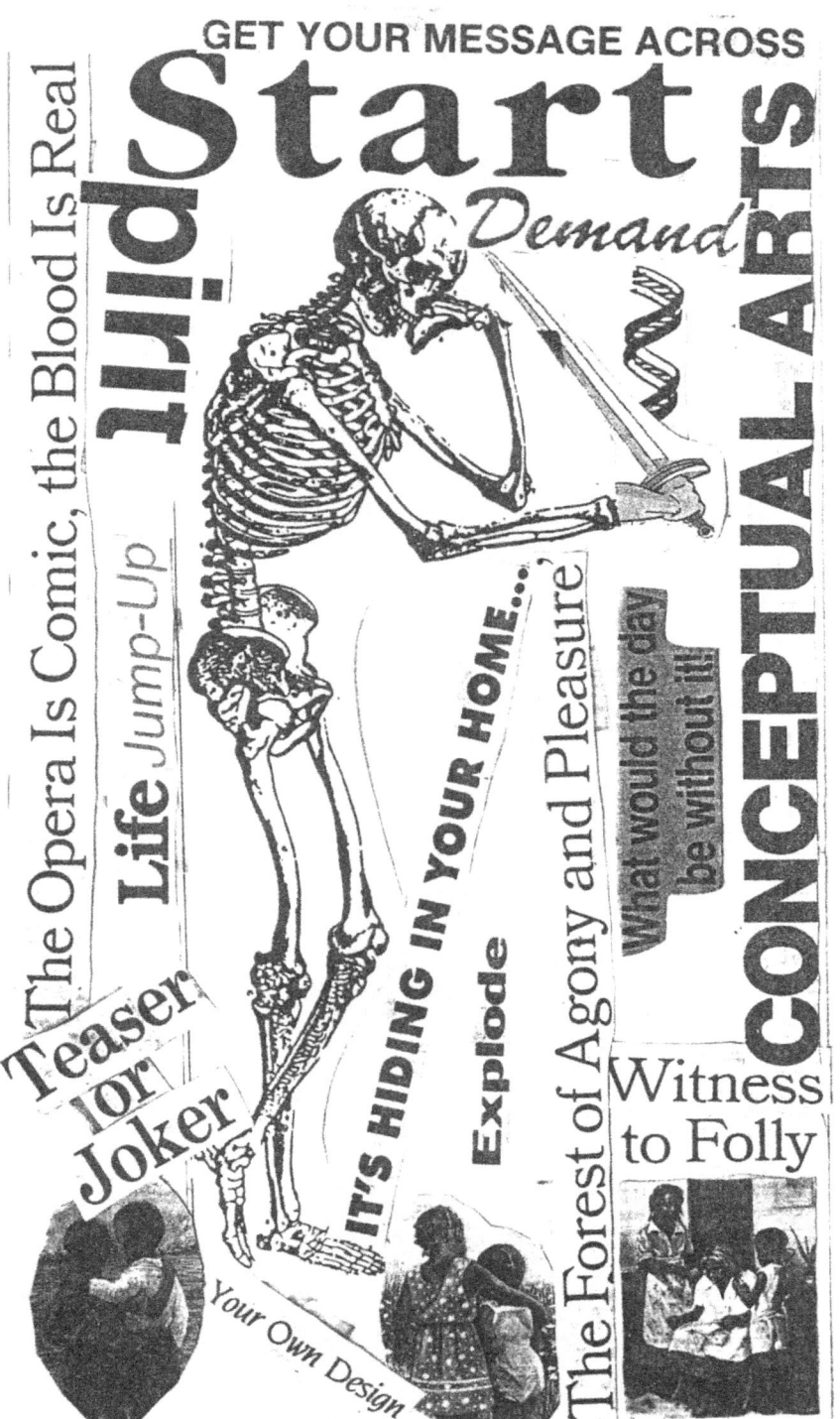

GET YOUR MESSAGE ACROSS

Start

Demand

Spirit

The Opera Is Comic, the Blood Is Real

Life Jump-Up

Teaser or Joker

IT'S HIDING IN YOUR HOME...

Explode

The Forest of Agony and Pleasure

What would the day be without it!

CONCEPTUAL ARTS

Witness to Folly

Your Own Design

Belief in a Compartment of My Heart

(for Ed Parrish)

You were the part
That kept me whole—
A link to my soul's line
Defining me.
Today, you achieved rebirth
On Earth
And turned into an element
Meant for everlasting
Green grass,
All trees
Caressing the spatial splendor
Of the aether,
All water
Rolling in Nature's eternally
Maternal flow,
And all things not of the flesh
But the infinite that
My thoughts cannot conceive.
This, in opposition to reason, is what
I believe.

The Jazzoetry Man

(for Louis Reyes Rivera)

Make Brother Rivera's

vida anew

in his Brooklyn barrio.

Trim his silver-

arranged mane

and plant the man's strands

in Mount Prospect Park.

The soil ought to say

it appreciates

venerated DNA.

Make it perceive our need

to reincarnate our late

poeta del pueblo.

Explain how this herdsman's words

served us.

Make it see why our eyes

and ears will need

his insights that invigorate

a page or a stage.

We want his audio

wisdom on the radio.

That oration is what

memory banks should stow.

Make the soil understand this:

For each day we live,

our souls need his perspective.

Father Teacher

(for Abba Elethea)

Often, in between staring

at your book's spine,

I remember the tenets

within its contents.

Ever and ever,

your versified endeavor,

replete with imagism

that rivals Jean Toomer's,

remains on my shelf.

It is a map to a place

where I find alchemical wealth,

which empowers my Black self.

Still the Messenger

Though Gil Scott-Heron
Would prefer
I not ride
The next train
In my cerebral subway
Along his ill-reputed route,
The tale's worthy of a tribute.

I can see
What's left of him:
An old Applejack-hat-wearing
Phantom
By his unstacked crack vials,
The booze he lived to use
Right beside the armrest arrest record,
And the grave-bringer cigarettes
Between his lips.

Then I remember him
Handing skepticism
A rhythm
By reciting revolutionary verses
That will outlast
Any program's broadcast,
Forever influencing rappers' jams
And poetry slams.

Anyplace Alienation Drinks

Charles Bukowski,
a leech for libations
once armed with pain,
a typewriter,
and pixilated viewpoints,
these days
goes to the Pantheon Taproom
with Dvořák
and Rimbaud for free rounds.

If there are
liquor-marred barflies
and the delusion that alcohol
forestalls tall problems,
Charles will dwell
anyplace alienation drinks.

Take a
Slow Train to
the Reaper

Thought-Steering on the Atmosphere

From my mountain-high rooftop view of the city, lights beam with starry regalness. Planes sail the cloud-clad road and go everywhere beyond my limited journeys. Above the street, I'm titan-tall on this summer night. But on the concrete, I'm another insect fleeing assassinating shoes. Fearing my place within that reality, I dream about remaining up here for the duration of a tree's persistent life. Far away from rushing and pushing commuters, I'm free.

Aware of another surveyor, I stare heavenward and find the moon wearing a pensive expression. Perhaps the orb examines our earthen kind, thinking, *I see you scrutinizing me, but what are you to me?* Now, resulting from persistent inspection, I see the moon's countenance conveying contempt for its isolation. Though the sphere veils days, summons tides, inspires wolf-howling madness, and makes oceans sway, no power unlatches its prison cell loneliness. Then, at last, by putting lunacy aside, I no longer want to anthropomorphize.

Clouds roll by this tar beach, and I watch the night exit behind a flaxen curtain. The sight makes me understand that a person's disposition determines beauty. This awareness gives me the mettle to handle what awaits below.

The Prevailing Success in Failure

"Dr. Arnold M. Ludwig looked at more than 1,000 prominent people in eight creative arts professions and ten other professions. He concluded that psychiatric disturbances were much more common among the artists. Dr. Ludwig found that roughly 20 percent of eminent poets had committed suicide, compared with a suicide rate of 4 percent for all the professions he examined."—from "Going Early Into That Good Night," a New York Times article by Felicia R. Lee

Fog banks obscured sane notions.
An indigo haze seeped out of my heart.
I found the cure over the counter:
myriad acetaminophen,
offering a mitigating miracle in childproof bottles.
The bliss of sedation's oblivion
made me rigor-mortis-motionless.

Feeling listless
within the purgatorial abyss,
I saw a phantasmagoria
of my poetic forebears.
I heard Hart Crane gasp
for his last breath
and joined Sylvia Plath
in *The Bell Jar*,
only to realize Parker's
"Résumé" was right.
"You might as well live."

Slow Train to the Reaper

Don't be the next one

who goes anchor-downward to drown.

Don't be the next one

who uses noxious gases for a grave.

Don't be the next one

to consume car fumes.

Don't be the next one

who gets undone by your gun.

Stay here.

Age for sagaciousness.

Remain alive.

Existence is a bestseller.

A Belated Message for the Ill-fated 27 Club

Musical rebels, you felt like infidels.

Even though the daughters of Zeus

unchained your emotional truth

and let you run loose to communicate the abuse

endured over the years,

their effort did not stop your tears.

Your songs of alienation and longing

got adoring multitudes,

but the real message in the lyrics

and notes eluded them.

Thus, your selfhood wandered

everywhere in the manner of a *flâneur*,

never finding a terminus anywhere.

Invariably, you surmised

that peace was in a drug-induced demise.

Then you became an unstrung artist,

à la the poet Thomas Chatterton.

In the end, musical rebels,

you left many yearning

for what your burning talent

could have created

beyond 27 complicated years.

Silver but not Blue

Time sucks the juice out of us.
Russell-viper-ravenous,
it will sup heads
until they're gray or hairless.
 It rends the senses
and jettisons them
without a destination.
It parks marks
on everything from our brows
to areas nearer the ground.
But those lines are badges
honoring our survival,
and those experiences become tutorials
for anyone able to listen.

GRIEF

STRESS

DEPRESSION

YOU ARE NOT ALONE!

"I think, therefore I am."

--Descartes

A Pertinacious
Philosophy

Ubiquitously You

You think the sun is laughing at your inability to rise. Your clock seems equally jocular, chortling between bells. Each annoying tintinnabular sound cannot rouse you. The attempts are useless. Coffin-lid-rigid, you continue lying on your bed. Unconcerned with the alarm, you await the ferry back to unconsciousness.

Later, after getting up and cleansing your mouth, you have the caffeine your brain and body deem essential. No matter the attempts at memorization, you cannot recall the day coffee shared the importance of air, food, and shelter. Once every drop gets pumped into your gullet, you turn into a car getting primed on premium.

Everything is rote for you. Diurnally, you shower at a specific hour. Then, in front of the bathroom mirror, you scrutinize your nude body.

You dress. Frequently, you look at the labels on your clothes. Not one garment is anonymous or generic. Each has a designation worthy of a phone book. In spite of that, you do not understand why designers decide what apparel is appropriate.

Fully clad, you commute. Any travel mode will do, provided it moves at speeds matching a cheetah, Usain Bolt, the Kawasaki Ninja H2, the Bugatti Veyron Super Sport, the CRH380A, or anything faster. You must reach a destination your heart detests quickly. Admit that a lobotomy and lodgings in a mental asylum would be better than the madness of racing to a place you wish were on the wrong side of a wrecking ball.

If given a chance, you would not work. Thus far, until you come into an inheritance, win the lottery, or rob a bank, you are stuck in the workforce. Such is the tale of an adult who has to bench press bills, and what a weight it is. You have the planet Jupiter's weight in debts.

You arrive. From 9 to 5, your employer incarcerates you. Very soon, whatever ideas of independence and confidence endure imprisonment. Granted, you will get paid, but it never seems like enough for the handcuffs on your individuality.

Halfway past the entrance, you see other people waiting for the elevator. Faced with finite options, you greet them and ask how they are. It is perfunctory. You do not care. Quite honestly, they do not care about you either. Old indoctrination from parents and teachers transforms everyone into parrots that say, "Good morning. How are you? Have a nice day." What you want to tell them is, *Until the votes come in, I can't tell if the morning is good or not. That should tell you how I am. And come to think of it, the day would be nicer if we didn't share greetings.*

Never forget the annoying weather spectators. You tolerate their need to editorialize about fluctuations. Repeatedly, they complain when it is either hot or cold, knowing full well that protestation cannot make a deity adjust the temperature to their requested specifications. Therefore, you fantasize about saying, *Weather the damn weather, complaining about it is the equivalent of pitching pebbles at a military tank. It is futile.*

Along with others, you ride the elevator. Amidst faces that fell to the floor long ago, you empathize with lobsters in a bucket. Experiencing claustrophobia, you want to yell about the width of your hatred for the job. You gripe to yourself and suppress your screams. Not content to merely stand, you notice the floor selection buttons. Irony's long feathers tickle your armpits. Considering the misfortune of employment, it seems farcical that there is no number thirteen. To trigger someone's triskaidekaphobia, you want to paint those disturbing digits on the walls.

Your floor appears. You arrive at work. The clock says, *You're late.* Any attempt at sneaking to your desk is a waste of subterfuge. Your employer sees you. Save your imagined Ninja skills for sneaking to the water cooler or the bathroom. None of the behindhand minutes make that superior any happier about your presence. Infantilized by that individual's reproaching look, you walk inside.

Of course, you know your boss, but in fantasies, that person takes on other appearances. Depending on how distraught your thoughts are, the authoritative figure can be any historical dictator, a police dog, or a demon right out of scripture.

Co-workers, a few of whom you tolerate, are measuring you for an asbestos suit. Honestly, you are about a cyberslacking second from a funeral pyre. Contrary to your physical mass, you are a non-refundable bottle, an object seen and unwanted. Except for their bobblehead motions of acknowledgment, no one cares that you are present. You do not speak; instead, your body imitates the famous drinking bird toy. Dejected, you squat behind your desk, where other annoyances congregate.

There you are doing what your imagination despises, which is work. Why mention what kind? A classification will not make the task any more likable.

At the very least, despite the job's attempts at editing out your individuality, you maintain your mind's original manuscript. This is your narrative. These experiences will be another edition on the bookshelf of existence. Grant yourself a favorable review, knowing your life will wind up out of print.

The Recipe to be a Writer

Besides a pencil or pen,

Paper, and imagination,

You need the ears of a moth,

An avian's vision,

A philomath's brain,

A Hippocratic heart,

And an empath's spirit.

Then mix in incidents from your life.

Let it all simmer,

And you'll write.

You'll write.

Beatnik Minds for Modern Times

To be a Beat poet,

you must travel roads

searching for the unknown

in yourself

and move with the speed

of Dean Moriarty.

See art everywhere,

from the gutter or the ether,

via a Proustian way

for a tire-sized novel

and any Blakean lay.

Go mad and use anaphoric

Whitmanesque lines

about polemics.

Yawp about a generation

and its unsung creations.

Wail about it till you sound close

to a Coltrane solo.

Remember, you can alchemize

the first thought you realize.

With the frequency of each sunrise,

improvise like Bob Kaufman.

And if your work gets published by a press

famous for its streetlight brightness,

you must forever remain Zen-egoless.

A Pertinacious Philosophy

Regardless of whether

your being's balloon is

touching the troposphere

or deflating on the salt flats,

continue to write.

If you are as dour

as a mourner,

write about it.

If your days

possess the jubilation

that a lottery winner knows,

write about it.

Chronicle who and what you are

before you are no more.

In the rental home

known as life,

remember the pending end

of your lease.

Therefore, before relocating to a necropolis,

create at the rate rabbits procreate.

Calendars do not determine your days.

The number of poems, stories,

essays, drawings, and performances

define your time as an artist.

From my point of view,

all artists should use that approach

as time encroaches.

Itinerary

The first verse
of this poem
birthed two legs.
Those legs are now
sprinting to a place
that you know.

The second verse
of this poem
bought a ten-speed bike.
That bike is now racing
to a place
that you know.

The last verse
of this poem
rented a car.
That car is now
darting to a place
where your heart
houses care.

Though the trip takes time,
this creation longs
for an invitation there.

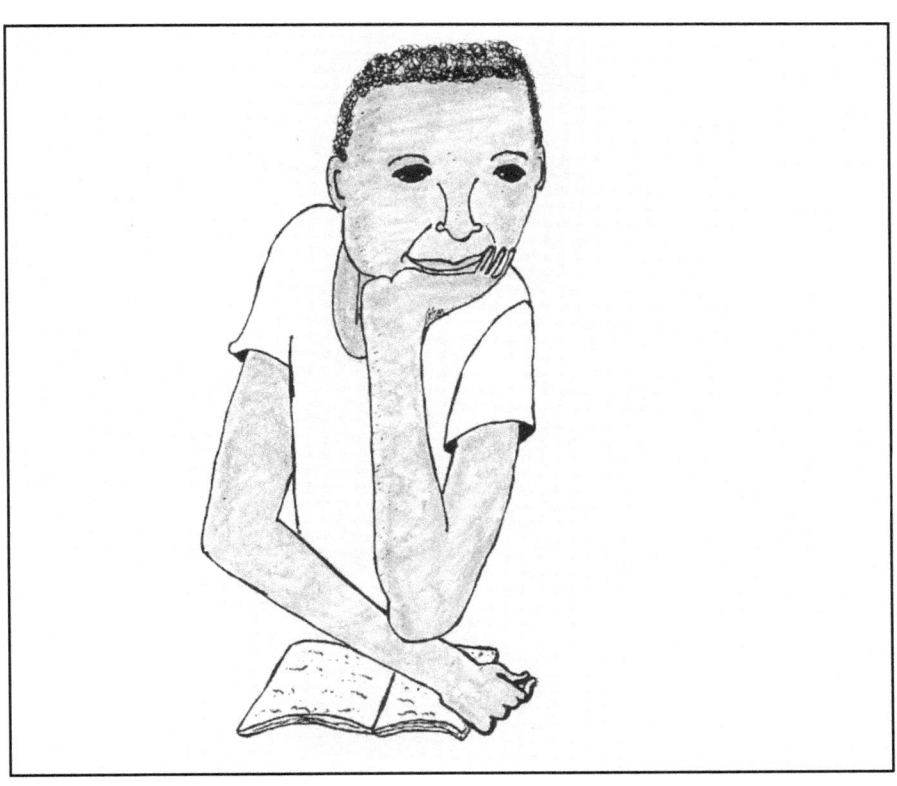

About the Author

Bob McNeil, writer, editor, and spoken word artist, is the author of *Verses of Realness*. Hal Sirowitz, a Queens Poet Laureate, called the book "a fantastic trip through the mind of a poet who doesn't flinch at the truth." Among Bob's recent accomplishments, he found working on *Lyrics of Mature Hearts* to be a humbling experience because of the anthology's talented contributors.

On the same level that Bob adores art, literature, and the company of a romantic, cerebral person, he treasures privacy. And youthful wanderlust taught him a valuable thing for his senior years: sharing sedentary comfort with a loved one has more value than the myriad social engagements beyond home's confines.

www.ingramcontent.com/pod-product-compliance
Lightning Source LLC
Chambersburg PA
CBHW041517120626
46551CB00018B/2472